SCHIRMER'S LIBRARY
OF MUSICAL CLASSICS

Vol. 50

J. B. DUVERNOY

Op 176

École Primaire

Twenty-Five Elementary Studies

For the Piano

G. SCHIRMER, Inc.

DISTRIBUTED BY
HAL•LEONARD
CORPORATION
7777 W. BLUEMOUND RD. P.O. BOX 13819 MILWAUKEE, WI 53213

Ecole primaire.

STUDY I.

J. B. DUVERNOY. Op. 176, Book 1.

Allegro moderato.

Piano.

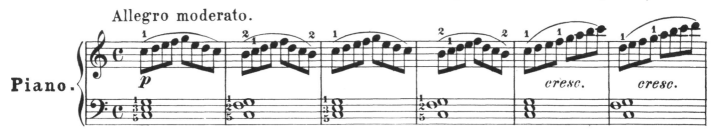

STUDY II.

Moderato.

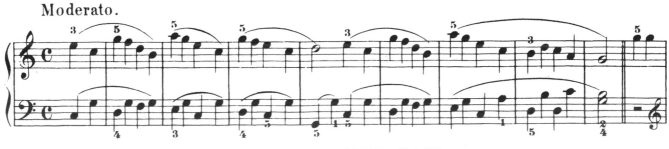

STUDY III.

Moderato.

STUDY IV.

Moderato.

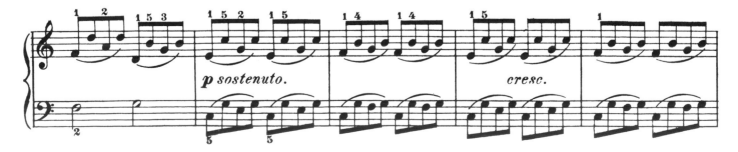

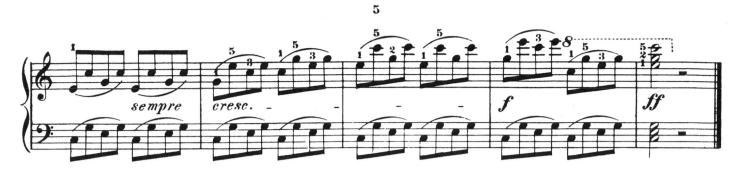

STUDY V.

Allegro moderato.

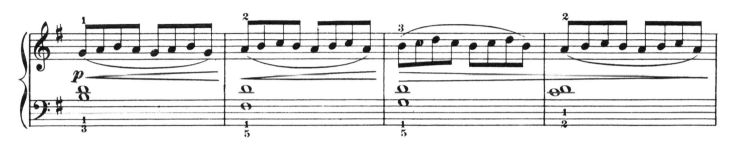

STUDY VI.

Andante.

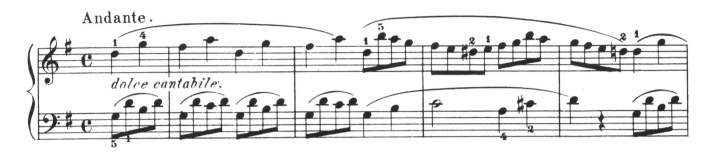

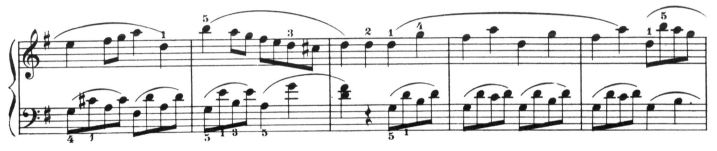

STUDY VII.

Moderato.

STUDY VIII.

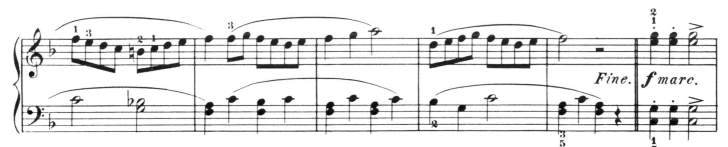

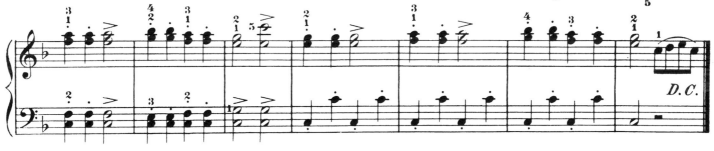

STUDY IX.

STUDY X.

Andantino.

STUDY XI.

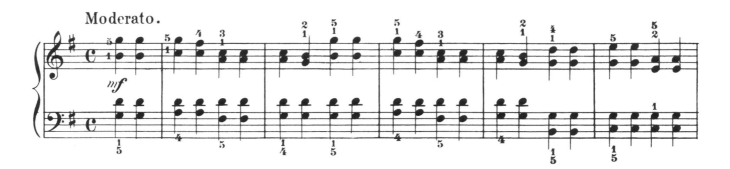

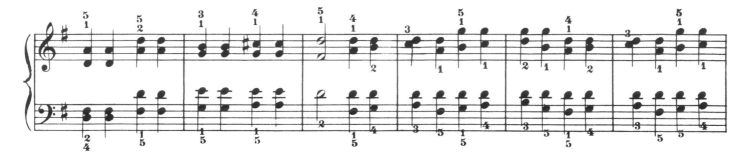

STUDY XII.

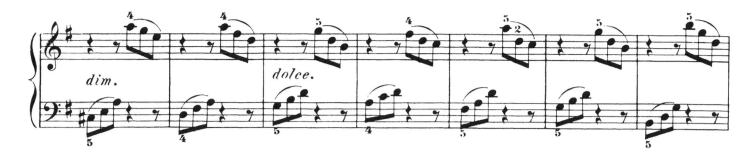

Ecole primaire.
STUDY XIII.

J. B. DUVERNOY. Op.176, Book 2.

Allegro commodo.

Piano.

STUDY XIV.

Allegro moderato.

STUDY XV.

Andantino.

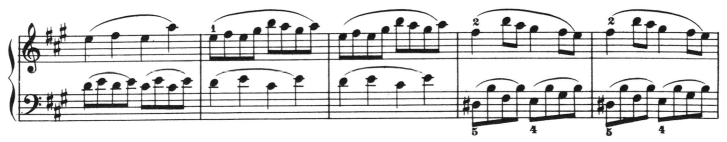

STUDY XVI.

Allegretto.

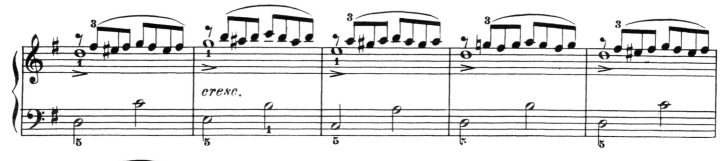

STUDY XVII.

Tempo di Valse.

STUDY XVIII.

Allegretto.

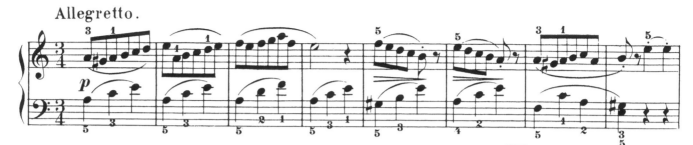

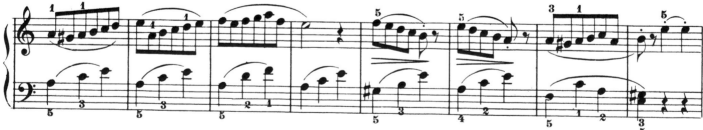

STUDY XIX.

Andante.

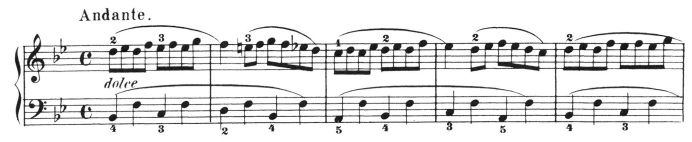

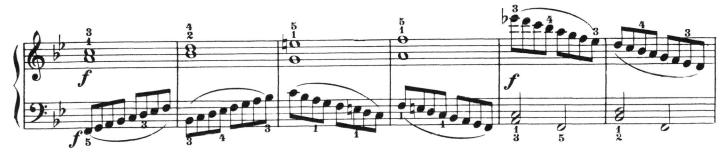

STUDY XX.

Allegro commodo.

STUDY XXI.

Moderato.

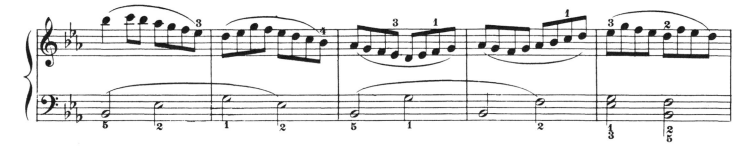

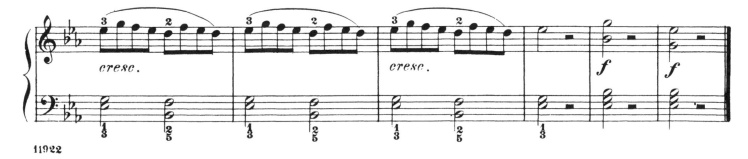

STUDY XXII.

Allegro, ma non troppo.

STUDY XXIII.

Allegretto.

D.C.

STUDY XXIV.

Allegretto

STUDY XXV.

Fanfare.